POST-TRAUMATIC STRESS DISORDER

Intrusion Symptoms • Avoidance Symptoms
Problems with Food, Thought, and Memory

H. W. Poole

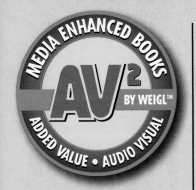

AV² provides enriched content that supplements and complements this book. Weigl's AV² books strive to create inspired learning and engage young minds in a total learning experience.

Your AV² Media Enhanced books come alive with...

Audio
Listen to sections of the book read aloud.

Key Words
Study vocabulary, and complete a matching word activity.

Video
Watch informative video clips.

Quizzes
Test your knowledge.

Embedded Weblinks
Gain additional information for research.

Slide Show
View images and captions, and prepare a presentation.

Try This!
Complete activities and hands-on experiments.

... and much, much more!

Go to **www.av2books.com,** and enter this book's unique code.

BOOK CODE

AVC93232

AV² by Weigl brings you media enhanced books that support active learning.

Published by AV² by Weigl
350 5th Avenue, 59th Floor
New York, NY 10118
Website: www.av2books.com

Library of Congress Control Number: 2018941343

ISBN 978-1-4896-7934-5 (hardcover)
ISBN 978-1-4896-7935-2 (softcover)
ISBN 978-1-4896-7936-9 (multi-user eBook)

Printed in Brainerd, Minnesota, United States
1 2 3 4 5 6 7 8 9 0   22 21 20 19 18

072018
120817

Project Coordinator: Heather Kissock Designer: Ana María Vidal

Every reasonable effort has been made to trace ownership and to obtain permission to reprint copyright material. The publisher would be pleased to have any errors or omissions brought to its attention so that they may be corrected in subsequent printings.

Weigl acknowledges Getty Images, iStock, Shutterstock, and Alamy as its primary image suppliers for this title.

First published by Mason Crest in 2016.

Contents

Bill was a soldier in Iraq for 18 months. During his time there, he and his fellow soldiers were in danger almost constantly. They saw terrible things that no person should have to see. When Bill's tour of duty ended, he was eager to get home to his wife and children. He could not wait to leave the ugliness of war behind. Once the joy of his homecoming wore off, though, Bill was not the same person anymore.

Before the war, Bill had been quite a patient guy. Now, his temper was short and explosive. It seemed like anything could send him into a rage, such as his son's toys on the floor, an overcooked steak, anything. Each night, he would have dreams about being in the middle of battle again. The nightmares got so bad that Bill tried to avoid going to sleep at all.

After the joy of homecoming, members of the armed forces have to cope with the challenges of civilian life.

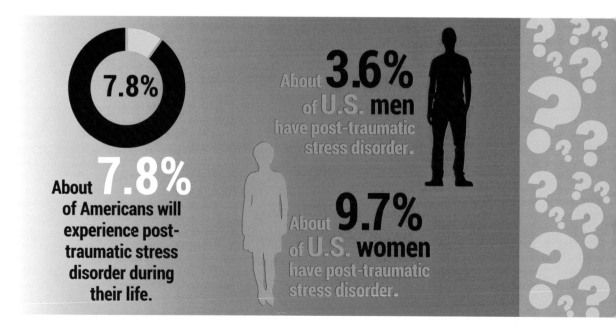

7.8%

About **7.8%** of Americans will experience post-traumatic stress disorder during their life.

About **3.6%** of U.S. men have post-traumatic stress disorder.

About **9.7%** of U.S. women have post-traumatic stress disorder.

About 30 percent of the men and women who have spent time in war zones experience PTSD.

Traumatic Experiences

Even when Bill was not angry, he was not happy. Nothing seemed to really matter to him. His wife worried about him. His children were often afraid. Bill had left the war, but the war had not left him.

Bill has a classic case of post-traumatic **stress** disorder (PTSD). PTSD is a mental disorder, but it is different from most other disorders in at least one very important way. When someone suffers from **anxiety** or **depression**, doctors often do not know exactly why. The cause may be physical, emotional, or some mix of the two. With PTSD, the cause is clear. It is trauma.

The Evolution of PTSD

The *Diagnostic and Statistical Manual of Mental Disorders* (*DSM*) was first published in 1952. The *DSM* is the official reference book for mental health professionals. It lists all the different types of mental disorders and explains the symptoms of each. The field of **psychiatry** is still evolving, and doctors' understanding of mental illness has changed over time. As doctors learn more about the human mind, they need to adjust the definitions of certain illnesses. For that reason, the *DSM* has been revised five times. The most recent edition, the *DSM-5*, was published in 2013.

Each edition has treated PTSD quite differently. The first edition referred to trauma reactions as "gross stress reaction." The second edition left out PTSD altogether, perhaps because it was written in peacetime. In the most recent edition, PTSD and related disorders have their own chapter, which is called "Trauma- and Stressor-Related Disorders."

TYPES OF TRAUMA

It has been estimated that as many as 60 percent of Americans will experience some form of trauma in their lives.

Examples of trauma include:

- military combat
- a violent crime
- a natural disaster
- a serious car accident
- the sudden death of a close family member or friend

A trauma is an upsetting event, but it is more than that. It is an event that is more extreme than most people experience. The experiences that Bill had in Iraq are not "regular" human experiences. Constantly fearing for his life, killing people, seeing people killed, these are all intense, horrifying experiences. They are often impossible to forget.

The Natural Order of Things

If a grandparent dies, that is very upsetting. However, the loss of an elderly person is an expected part of life. People might say it is the "natural order of things." It is important to understand that saying this does not mean the loss is insignificant. You might be extremely upset and miss your grandparent for a very long time. It is just not what a doctor would describe as a trauma.

On the other hand, the death of a sister or a brother probably would be described as a trauma. The death of a sibling is not part of the "natural order of things." It is outside what people would call regular or normal human experience.

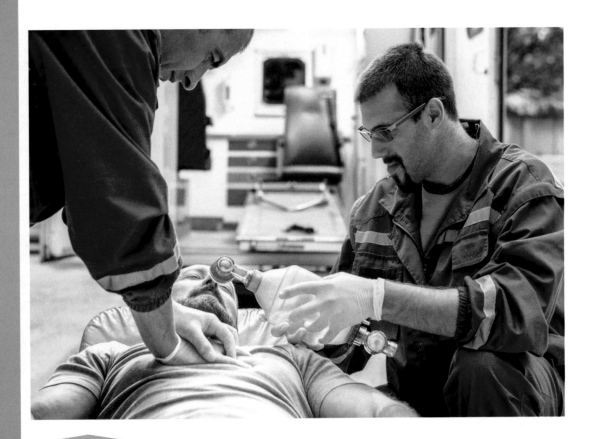

The trauma of a serious accident can bring about PTSD in the injured person.

Another key indicator of trauma is the level of stress the person experiences. You might feel stress before you take a test or if you get in trouble with your parents. If you compare taking a test to fighting in a battle, though, your level of stress is actually fairly low. Also, it will pass once the test is over. On the other hand, the **acute** stress that people feel during a trauma can take a long time to go away. It can have long-term effects on the brain. This is why people who have experienced trauma sometimes re-experience that trauma again and again.

Defining Normal

An explanation of the word "trauma" only raises another issue. If trauma is outside of "normal" human experience, then what is normal has to be defined. In some instances, normal is easy to define. If someone is mugged on the way home from work, that is not normal. Millions of people travel to and from work every day without getting mugged. A lot of times, the definition of normal depends on **context**.

Consider the example of the death of a sibling. If someone is 90 years old and her brother is 89, the death of either one is, although still sad, not unexpected. If someone is 12 years old, though, and her brother is 9, it is not normal for either of them to die. So the death of a sibling could be a "normal" event or not, depending on the person.

In the example of Bill the soldier, fighting in a war is not a "normal" experience for him. That is, it is not normal in many parts of the world. In some parts of the world, though, it is not uncommon at all.

A shocking and distressing event, such as experiencing a break-in, can be so traumatic that the homeowner later develops PTSD.

Warfare is the type of trauma most closely associated with PTSD. After the American Civil War (1861–1865), soldiers like Bill were said to have "soldier's heart." People do not have to be soldiers to experience trauma, though. Unfortunately, lots of people have soldier's hearts. The history of PTSD shows that it was first identified in **veterans**, but doctors today are finding signs of PTSD in people who have never been in an actual war.

Take a Deeper Look

Ask people of varying ages, such as parents, teachers, friends, or older children, for permission to interview them about stress. Some questions you might ask include, "What makes you feel 'stressed out'?" "What do you do when you feel that way?" "Do you have any tricks to help calm down?" What do you notice about their answers? What aspects of their answers are similar or different?

② The History of PTSD

An ancient Greek historian named Herodotus described a general who refused to send some of his soldiers into battle. He could see they were too damaged mentally. "They had no heart for the fight," Herodotus wrote.

War and Trauma

In the past, many people assumed that soldiers who had "no heart for the fight" were weak or cowardly. In the Civil War novel *The Red Badge of Courage*, a young soldier named Henry Fleming runs away from battle and then feels guilty about having been a coward. Today, readers can recognize Fleming's anxiety and fear as being similar to what doctors now call PTSD.

The writings of Herodotus prove that even ancient wars were traumatic events. Yet the first detailed descriptions of war trauma did not begin to appear until after the Civil War. After World War I (1914–1918), those traumas appeared to be even worse and affect even more people.

Every war throughout history has been traumatic for the people who fought it. It was not until the late nineteenth century that war trauma began to be recognized.

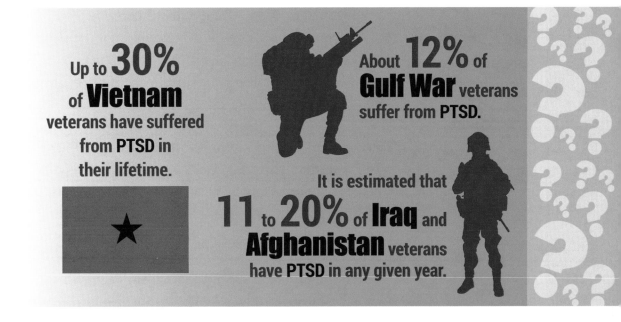

Up to **30%** of **Vietnam** veterans have suffered from PTSD in their lifetime.

About **12%** of **Gulf War** veterans suffer from PTSD.

It is estimated that **11** to **20%** of **Iraq** and **Afghanistan** veterans have PTSD in any given year.

Technology, which makes people's lives so much easier every day, also makes war "easier." The American Civil War killed more than 625,000 soldiers. An average of 420 soldiers died every day during the conflict. The Battle of Gettysburg, which took place in Pennsylvania in July 1863, resulted in 51,000 dead in just three days. The Battle of Chickamauga, in Georgia in September of the same year, claimed more than 34,000 lives in just two days. The emotional toll this must have taken on survivors is almost impossible to imagine today.

During World War I in Europe, more than 9 million soldiers were killed along with almost 7 million civilians. The United States fought in the war only at the end, from 1917 to 1918. About 116,000 U.S. soldiers died fighting overseas. In total, 16 million people died in a little more than four years, and another 21 million were wounded. These numbers are difficult to visualize. The reason that so much death took place in such a short time is technology.

World War I was the war of the tank and the flamethrower, of chlorine and mustard gas. It was the first war to use airplanes in combat. World War I was also the war of the machine gun. On the first day of the Battle of the Somme in France in 1916, more than 19,000 British soldiers died.

Trauma at Home

Technology did not only bring trauma to the battlefield. By the late nineteenth century, there were increasing numbers of machines in the workplace. Soon after, there were increasing numbers of cars on the streets. More people worked in industrial jobs and traveled in cars and trains.

The Cocoanut Grove Fire

In the early 1940s, the Cocoanut Grove nightclub was one of the most popular spots in Boston. People would crowd into the club to listen to big bands and dance. Safety laws were **lax** back then, and 1,000 or more people would crowd into a building that was designed to hold half that many. Tragedy struck on November 28, 1942, when a fire ripped through the building. Panicked customers discovered that the revolving doors had jammed, while other doors were locked. In the end, 492 people died.

The Cocoanut Grove fire remains the worst nightclub disaster in U.S. history. A number of positive things came out of the tragedy. New safety regulations were adopted. New techniques for treating burn victims were invented at Boston hospitals. Meanwhile, several **psychologists** did hugely important work. Erich Lindemann studied grieving families, while Alexandra Adler studied survivors. She found that even a year after the fire, survivors were still experiencing extreme guilt, personality changes, sleep problems, and anxiety. Her writings on their struggles helped other doctors understand how PTSD can affect civilians.

All these developments of the **Industrial Revolution** were positive in many ways, but they also had a dark side. For example, the English writer Charles Dickens was a survivor of the Staplehurst train crash of 1865. Dickens blamed his "unsteady" feelings on the actual shaking of the train car during the accident. Modern doctors would be much more likely to blame the mental trauma. "I am curiously weak," Dickens wrote, "as if I were recovering from a long illness."

It may be that doctors recognized PTSD in soldiers because the wartime experience is so extreme. A soldier leaves home as one person, but due to the trauma of battle, that soldier sometimes comes home a very different person. As the experience of Charles Dickens reveals, though, PTSD has also probably been in the civilian world for a long time.

Medical Views of PTSD

PTSD has gone by a variety of names. In addition to "soldier's heart," the term "nervous shock" came into use in the late nineteenth century. The cause of nervous shock was often thought to be physical. The English physician John Eric Erichsen wrote about patients who were "subject to the violent shock of railway collision," and he argued that spinal injuries were causing the symptoms.

Not only passengers but also transit workers can suffer from PTSD after an accident. Federal regulations were put in place in 2014 so that U.S. railroad companies have to address the mental health needs of employees after accidents.

The term "railway spine" became a common way to describe this problem. However, there was a school of thought, even at this early stage, that held the symptoms were related to what doctors used to call hysteria. The term "hysteria" is an outdated term for anxiety, and doctors no longer use it. Even in the late nineteenth century, though, some doctors were wondering if "nervous shock" could be mental, rather than physical.

After World War I, thousands of soldiers spent time in hospital recovering not only from physical wounds and illness but also from emotional trauma.

The World Wars

The horrors of World War I made this debate even more urgent. In 1915, a British Army doctor named Charles Myers published the first major article on what he called "shell shock." By the end of the war, British officials had counted 80,000 cases. Symptoms of shell shock included nightmares, sudden violent thoughts, insomnia, and severe anxiety. Sufferers also had physical problems that were very difficult to explain. For example, a soldier who had been a **sniper** would suddenly become blind for no physical reason. Another soldier might have constant diarrhea but no other sign of physical illness.

World War II expanded medical interest in shell shock. In this war, the disorder came to be known as "battle fatigue." As many as half of World War II veterans are believed to have experienced some level of battle fatigue.

Chapter 3

Symptoms of PTSD

eople's understanding of trauma has changed since World War I. Today, it is clear that a person does not have to be a solider to experience trauma. In fact, he or she does not even have to be a grownup. The *DSM-5* has an entire chapter dedicated to trauma-related disorders, and it lists slightly different symptoms for children under six than it does for older children and adults.

Classic PTSD

When doctors **diagnose** PTSD, they rely on the definition of the disorder given in the *DSM-5*. That definition has a number of categories.

STRESSOR. The word "stressor" is another term for the traumatic experience that caused the symptoms in the first place. There are different types of stressors. A stressor could be war, violent crime, a natural disaster, or some other event. There are also different ways to experience stressors.

People do not all have the same reactions to an experience. An event can be traumatic for one person but not at all traumatic for another.

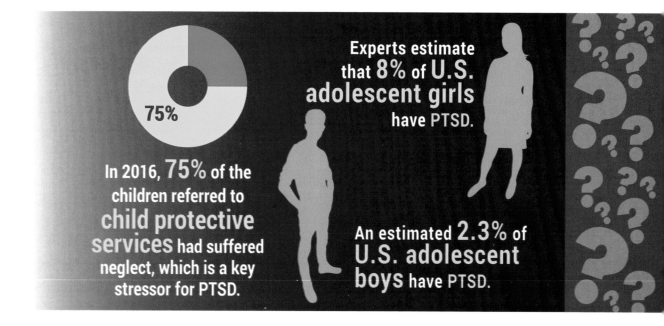

75%

In 2016, 75% of the children referred to **child protective services** had suffered neglect, which is a key stressor for PTSD.

Experts estimate that 8% of U.S. **adolescent girls** have PTSD.

An estimated 2.3% of **U.S. adolescent boys** have PTSD.

You could be directly affected by the stressor by being, for example, the victim of a violent crime.

You could witness someone else being affected by seeing a violent crime take place.

You could learn about someone you love being affected by hearing that your parent was the victim of a violent crime.

You could be repeatedly affected by traumas that happen to others, such as those who work in jobs touched by trauma.

People in law enforcement are at risk of PTSD because they are exposed to trauma in their jobs.

These four types of exposure can all have different impacts on different people. Some children might be traumatized by hearing about a school shooting, while other kids could hear the same story and not find it traumatic. Neither reaction is right or wrong. Different people can respond differently to the same stressor.

INTRUSION SYMPTOMS. People with PTSD keep thinking about the stressor again and again, even when they do not want to. This is called an **intrusion** symptom. Nightmares and **flashbacks**, which are like waking nightmares, are common. People with PTSD can also get very upset when something reminds them of the traumatic event. For example, the sound of a car backfiring might remind a veteran of the gunshots she used to hear on the battlefield. At that moment, she might feel like she is in the middle of the war again, even though she is safe at home.

TYPES OF TRAUMA DISORDERS

Doctors' understanding of PTSD has come a long way from the days when traumatized soldiers were shamed for their "cowardice." The *DSM-5* not only includes PTSD but also other trauma-related disorders.

Reactive attachment disorder. This type of disorder can affect both adults and children. The problem arises in very young children when some trauma prevents them from developing healthy bonds with caregivers. In adults, it is the inability to form loving and lasting relationships, to give or receive affection or trust others.

Disinhibited social engagement disorder. This disorder is found more in children than in adults. It can occur when a trauma, which is often severe neglect, causes children to be too outgoing or aggressive with people they do not know. Children with this disorder will often go off with any adult, whether that person can be trusted or not.

Acute stress disorder. This type of disorder can affect both adults and children. It is very similar to PTSD, but it occurs almost immediately after the traumatic event and tends not to last as long as PTSD.

Although it is not in the *DSM-5*, some doctors have argued for one more diagnosis to be included. Called complex post-traumatic stress disorder (C-PTSD), this new diagnosis would relate to trauma that goes on for a long time, such as many years of abuse. Some doctors believe that traumas lasting for years result in different problems than brief traumas such as car accidents.

AVOIDANCE SYMPTOMS. People with PTSD will often work very hard to stay away from anything that reminds them of their trauma. There is nothing wrong with trying to avoid feeling bad. However, this avoidance can get to the point when it makes daily life very difficult. For example, a veteran might **associate** the smell of gasoline with his time on the battlefield. The smell of gasoline becomes a **trigger** for the veteran's PTSD. He might want to do anything to avoid the smell. That is not a big problem until his car runs out of gas. At that point, his avoidance symptoms are interfering with his desire to have a normal life.

For veterans, sudden and loud noises, such as fireworks, can trigger an episode of PTSD.

PROBLEMS WITH MOOD, THOUGHT, AND MEMORY. In the weeks, months, and years after the traumatic event, people with PTSD can get depressed and angry for what seems like no reason at all. People with PTSD also tend to have very negative views of the world. In other words, instead of thinking, "sometimes bad things happen," someone with PTSD might think, "the entire world is bad and nothing good happens at all." They become **estranged** from friends and family, in part because those other people cannot understand their new, dark view of the world.

A survey found that depression is almost three to five times more likely in people with PTSD than those without the disorder.

Things to Avoid

The mental health website HelpGuide.org lists some suggestions of what *not* to say to someone with PTSD. It advises that people do not:

• give easy answers, like "everything is going to be okay"

• stop the person from talking about his or her feelings or fears

• tell the person what he or she "should" do

• blame all of your relationship or family problems on the person's PTSD

• minimize or deny the person's experience

• tell the person to "get over it" or "snap out of it"

• make threats or demands

• make the person feel weak because he or she is not coping as well as others

• tell the person he or she is lucky it was not worse

• take over the conversation with your own personal experiences or feelings

CHANGES IN ATTENTION LEVELS. People with PTSD are often irritated, and they often have trouble relaxing. This is due to a phenomenon called hypervigilance, in which someone is "on guard" all the time. All humans have what is called a fight-or-flight response to stressful situations. When people perceive a threat, their hearts beat faster, and they feel a jolt of energy. This is a survival skill that everyone is born with, and there is nothing wrong with it. People with PTSD can experience the fight-or-flight response at any time, even when there is no real threat.

People with PTSD also tend to have trouble concentrating on basic tasks. Sometimes they forget things easily. They particularly forget things that connect to their trauma.

Abuse and neglect are major stressors for PTSD in children. From 2012 to 2016, the number of U.S. children investigated by child protective services for maltreatment increased by 9.5 percent.

PTSD in Young Children

It is painful to think about young children dealing with PTSD. Unfortunately, being young is no protection from traumatic experiences. Very young kids can experience abuse, car accidents, and natural disasters just like older people do. Some children are neglected, and some grow up in extremely violent neighborhoods. These are all possible causes of PTSD in the very young.

Many PTSD symptoms are the same no matter how old the person is. There are a few aspects of PTSD in children, though, that are different. The most important one has to do with speech.

It is easy to take language for granted. However, if you do not know the word for a particular thing, it is very difficult to talk about that thing. It is even difficult to think about the thing in any real way. A two-year-old boy who has been rescued from a terrible fire, for example, probably knows a limited number of words. He has no way of explaining how scared he is. His reactions to surviving the fire might be confusing, both to him and to his parents.

He cannot "talk through" his experiences the way an older person would. Young children cannot say, "This upsets me." However, they do express themselves in different ways. It is for that reason that doctors pay less attention to words and more to behavior in young children. For example, over-the-top **tantrums** are common in children with PTSD. A flat **affect** is also common. Children with PTSD sometimes do not show the excitement or energy that one would expect in someone their age.

Nightmares

Nightmares also are common in young children with PTSD, just like they are with adults. However, the subject of the nightmare might not connect to the trauma in a direct way. A veteran might have nightmares about the war he survived. There will usually be a clear connection between the stressor and the dream. A young child might have more general nightmares that are not obviously related to the trauma. The two-year-old who was rescued from the fire might not even have clear memories of what happened during the trauma. He might have nightmares, but they might not be about fires.

Expression in Play

Young children might not be able to say what is wrong, but they can show it. One common way children work out their feelings is through play. A child who witnessed a violent crime might suddenly start treating her dolls in a way that reflects what she saw. When traumatized children are playing, they might act out the same scenario over and over. This is called repetitive play or reenactment.

Alternatively, traumatized children might play in a way that is less imaginative than most children their age. This is called constricted play. It may be a sign that stress from a trauma is weighing heavily on the child's mind. This makes it hard for them to engage with their imaginations as actively as other children.

Traumatized children may depict the trauma they have experienced in their drawings and paintings, which can help them process their traumatic memories.

Treating PTSD

People who develop PTSD can get better. There are several approaches to the treatment of PTSD. Which approach is best depends on the person and the nature of the problem.

Cognitive Processing Therapy

One way of thinking about PTSD is to say that the person has become "stuck" in the moment of the trauma. The person continues to re-experience the painful memories because he or she cannot quite make sense of them. One type of **therapy**, called **cognitive** processing therapy (CPT), helps people better understand the trauma and their reactions to it. In CPT, patients learn about what PTSD is and why they might have it. They try to become more aware of their reactions to and feelings about memories and triggers. They also learn new ways to cope with these feelings. CPT involves regular meetings with a therapist, as well as exercises to do outside of the doctor's office, to practice new skills.

It can be challenging for veterans, who have been trained to be "tough," to admit they have a problem with PTSD.

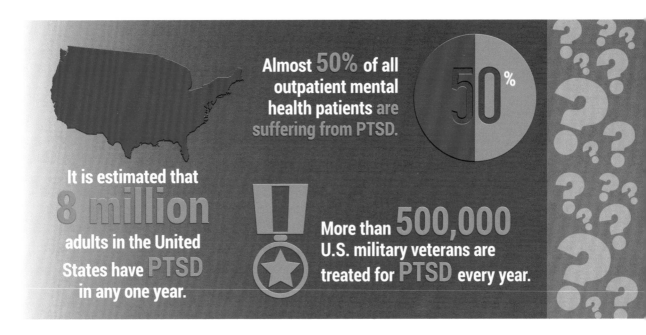

Almost 50% of all outpatient mental health patients are suffering from PTSD.

50%

It is estimated that 8 million adults in the United States have PTSD in any one year.

More than 500,000 U.S. military veterans are treated for PTSD every year.

Using CPT for PTSD

CPT has been shown to be very effective in treating PTSD sufferers. In CPT, the therapist examines what the traumatized person is thinking and telling himself about his trauma. She then decides whether those thoughts are accurate or inaccurate. For example, frequently people heap blame on themselves for the terrible things that happened, saying things like, "It's my fault that my buddy died." In CPT, therapists do not change the details of what happened. Rather, they change the things that the person is telling himself that are increasing his PTSD symptoms.

Prolonged Exposure Therapy

This type of therapy addresses the symptoms of anxiety and avoidance that are so common with PTSD. **Prolonged exposure therapy (PET)** involves talk therapy, relaxation exercises, and careful exposure to whatever triggers tend to cause the PTSD symptoms. For example, a veteran who experienced a bomb going off in a trash bin might, understandably, become anxious around trash cans. PET might be able to help that veteran understand and manage his anxiety, so that trash cans no longer trigger the PTSD.

Medication

One challenge with all the treatments is that they take some time to work. Also, the patient needs to be stable enough to be able to benefit from the treatment in the first place. For that reason, people suffering from severe PTSD will often be prescribed antidepressant or antianxiety medication. Usually, the patient will take the medicine for only a short time. The medicine does not "fix" PTSD. It helps patients feel well enough so that they can get involved in therapy.

In addition to individual therapy, group therapy can be helpful for people suffering from PTSD.

Living with PTSD

The challenges of living with the symptoms of PTSD are not always easy to cope with. There are some strategies to help manage the disorder that can improve the quality of life for people with PTSD and their loved ones.

Asking for Help

It is common for people with PTSD to withdraw into themselves, but connecting with others is extremely important.

Family Connections

Many treatment programs for veterans suffering from PTSD try to involve families and loved ones in treatment as well.

Helping Others

One way to feel better is to help others. Volunteer work, helping friends, and donating to charity are ways to connect with others.

Avoid Drugs and Alcohol

It is a bad idea to use drugs or alcohol just to cope. This will make the PTSD moods worse and increase feelings of helplessness.

Know the Triggers

It may not be possible to avoid the triggers for PTSD, but it is possible to be prepared for them and what may happen.

Patience and Understanding

There will be good days and bad days. No one is perfect. It is important to be understanding and patient with a PTSD sufferer.

PTSD over Time

PTSD has been around for all human history, and many great writers have described its symptoms. However, it is only in the last 150 years or so that society has been able to examine it openly to find the best ways of treating the disorder.

1865

English writer Charles Dickens was involved in a train crash in which 10 people were killed and many more were injured. Dickens was not hurt physically, but he described himself as "not quite right within." He never lost his fear of trains.

1914-1918

Soldiers suffering from PTSD during World War I were described as having "shell shock" or "war strain." Doctors recognized it as a common reaction to the stress of the battlefield. By the end of the war, the British Army had dealt with 80,000 cases of shell shock.

1943

In two separate incidents, General George Patton slapped soldiers who he felt were pretending to be unwell. The U.S. Army's official position was that "every man has his breaking point." Patton was suspended for months for his unsympathetic reaction to the men.

A mental health professional can advise on the best treatment plan to follow to manage PTSD.

1980

The American Psychiatric Association (APA) added PTSD to the third edition of its *Diagnostic and Statistical Manual of Mental Disorders* (*DSM-III*). It stated that an outside agent, a trauma, is the cause of the disorder, rather than a weakness in the individual.

AMERICAN
PSYCHIATRIC
ASSOCIATION

1989

The U.S. Department of Veterans Affairs opened a National Center for PTSD, nine years after the *DSM-III* defined the condition. It is dedicated to research and education on trauma and PTSD for veterans and their families, the public, and professionals.

2017

Researchers at Stellenbosch University in South Africa found a link between the bacteria in a person's gut and the likelihood of him or her developing PTSD after experiencing a traumatic event. Low levels of certain bacteria are associated with developing PTSD.

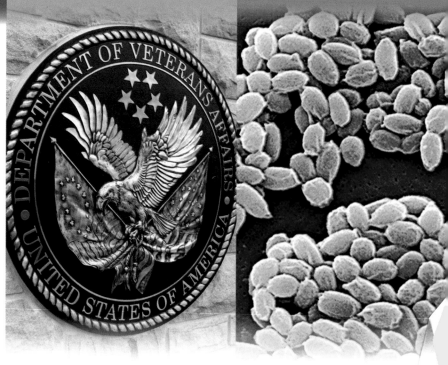

Quiz

1 What experience is most associated with PTSD?

2 What is the name of the ancient Greek who wrote about soldiers who had "no heart for the fight"?

3 What is the title of the novel about the Civil War in which a form of PTSD is described?

4 In what war did the term "shell shock" come to be used for PTSD?

5 Where did a fire take place in 1942 that was important in the study of PTSD?

6 Which U.S. general slapped soldiers suffering from PTSD in 1943?

7 What percentage of Americans will experience trauma at some point in their lives?

8 What is CPT?

9 When did the *Diagnostic and Statistical Manual of Mental Disorders* (*DSM*) first define PTSD?

10 What two types of medication are people with PTSD prescribed?

Key Words

acute: intense or severe

affect: as a noun, the way someone seems on the outside, attitude, emotion, and voice

anxiety: a feeling of worry or nervousness

associate: to link two things together in the mind

cognitive: having to do with the brain or thought

context: the larger situation in which an event occurs

depression: a feeling of hopelessness and lack of energy

diagnose: to identify a problem

estranged: no longer feeling close or affectionate toward someone

flashbacks: strong memories of a past event that come suddenly to mind

Industrial Revolution: a period starting in the late 1700s when power-driven machines made products cheaper and travel faster

intrusion: the appearance of something unwanted

lax: not strict

prolonged: going on for a long time

psychiatry: a field of medicine having to do with mental illness

psychologists: scientists who study the human mind and behavior

sniper: person who shoots at someone from a hidden position

stress: an emotion or condition involving tension and fear

tantrums: uncontrollable angry outbursts

therapy: the treatment of a problem. It can be done with medicine or simply by talking with a therapist.

trigger: cause something to happen

veterans: former members of the armed forces

Index

Log on to www.av2books.com

AV² by Weigl brings you media enhanced books that support active learning. Go to www.av2books.com, and enter the special code found on page 2 of this book. You will gain access to enriched and enhanced content that supplements and complements this book. Content includes video, audio, weblinks, quizzes, a slide show, and activities.

AV² Online Navigation

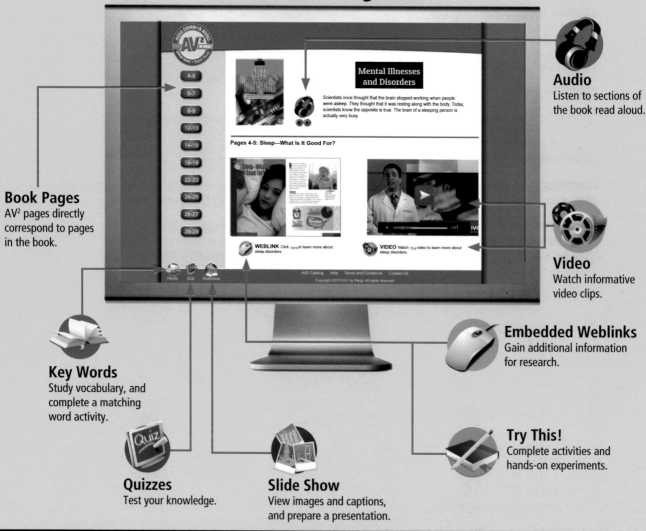

Audio
Listen to sections of the book read aloud.

Book Pages
AV² pages directly correspond to pages in the book.

Video
Watch informative video clips.

Key Words
Study vocabulary, and complete a matching word activity.

Embedded Weblinks
Gain additional information for research.

Quizzes
Test your knowledge.

Slide Show
View images and captions, and prepare a presentation.

Try This!
Complete activities and hands-on experiments.

AV² was built to bridge the gap between print and digital. We encourage you to tell us what you like and what you want to see in the future.

Sign up to be an AV² Ambassador at www.av2books.com/ambassador.